Beginner's Guide to

Berlin Woolwork

To my husband, Richard, and daughters Sarah and Lisa

Beginner's Guide to
Berlin Woolwork

Jane Alford

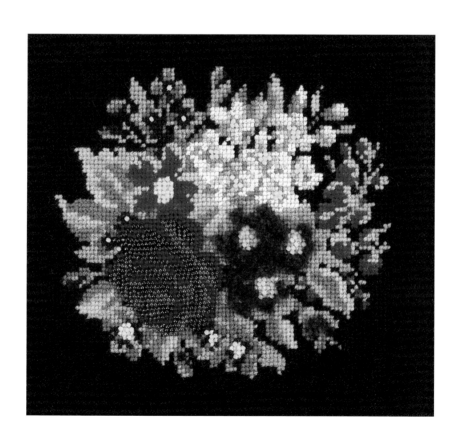

SEARCH PRESS

First published in Great Britain 2003

Search Press Limited
Wellwood, North Farm Road,
Tunbridge Wells, Kent TN2 3DR

Text copyright © Jane Alford 2003
Embroidery designs copyright © Jane Alford 2003

Photographs by Search Press Studios
Photographs and design copyright © Search Press Ltd. 2003

ISBN 0 85532 936 X

The Publishers and author can accept no responsibility for any
consequences arising from the information, advice or instructions
given in this publication.

Readers are permitted to reproduce any of the embroideries in this
book for their personal use, or for the purposes of selling for
charity, free of charge and without the prior permission of the
Publishers. Any use of the embroideries for commercial purposes is
not permitted without the prior permission of the Publishers.

Suppliers
If you have difficulty in obtaining any of the materials and
equipment mentioned in this book, then please write to the
Publishers, at the address above, for a current list of stockists,
including firms who operate a mail-order service.

Many thanks to Helen Burke for charting the
designs and to Phoebe Wright for stitching
some of the samples.
  Thanks also to DMC Creative World,
Pullman Road, Wigston, Leicester LE18 2DY
for providing all the wool, cotton, canvas and
beads, and to the Coleshill Collection,
Orchard House Industrial Estate, Amersham
Road, Chesham, Buckinghamshire HP5 1NE
for the Able Stretcher Frame.

Publisher's note
All the step-by-step photographs in this book feature the
author, Jane Alford, demonstrating Berlin woolwork
embroidery. No models have been used.

Printed in Spain by Elkar S. Coop. Bilbao 48012

Page 1

Bluebells
see page 42 for chart

Page 3

Floral Spray
see page 46 for chart

Page 5

Poppies
see page 40 for chart

Contents

INTRODUCTION

Berlin woolwork was worked on canvas, and was extremely fashionable and popular during the nineteenth century. Charted designs, which were mass-produced in Berlin, were an instant success. The stitches were in the main limited to tent and cross stitch, though pile stitch, which is also known as plush or velvet stitch, was sometimes used. Designs included flowers, exotic birds, animals and geometric patterns, and embroiderers would make rugs, stools, bell-pulls and fire screens.

Some of the earliest pieces were worked on a fine single mesh canvas, like the embroidery opposite, which was probably intended for use as a fire screen. It must have taken many hours to complete, and is worked with a combination of cross stitch and half cross stitch over one or two threads of canvas. The background was left un-worked, as was often the case when the canvas had a fine mesh. Silk thread and wool from Gremany were used for the embroidery.

The first charts were produced in the early 1800s, and by 1810 a Madame Wittich and her print maker husband started to print them on a commercial basis. The designs were produced by local artists, copied on to the canvas, then coloured by hand. Although flower and animal designs were available, the earliest charts of countryside scenes and geometric patterns were more popular.

Berlin woolwork charts were introduced to London in 1831 by a Mr. Wilks who opened an embroidery shop. They were so expensive that he bought them back from his rich clients after they had used them, and resold them to his less-wealthy clients at reduced prices. Embroiderers loved the hand-coloured designs and the brightly coloured wools that also came from Berlin, and they soon moved on from their more traditional ways of working. By the time Queen Victoria came to the throne in 1837 there were hundreds of patterns available. The social standing of a Victorian lady was greatly enhanced when she took up embroidery, which showed that she had servants to do all her chores, while she had enough leisure time to pursue other interests.

Today, with the amazing range of wools and colours available, embroiderers are able to recreate the vibrancy and beauty of the original designs that decorated Victorian parlours. I have tried to impart some of my enthusiasm and admiration for the beautiful embroideries of this bygone era in the following pages. I hope there is enough here to whet your appetite, so that as you stitch these treasures from the past you will experience as much pleasure as I have done.

Fire screen
This magnificent fire screen, an early piece of Victorian woolwork, is embroidered on a 24 count single thread silk canvas in a mix of cross stitch and tent stitch. The background of fine, good quality canvas is left un-sewn. The vibrant colours result from the use of a superior type of wool from Germany, which held the dye well. Combined with the brilliance of perlé cotton, this outstanding piece of needlework would have enhanced any Victorian parlour.

Materials & equipment

Before starting to embroider, it is important to equip yourself with the right tools. The next few pages show you what you will need to produce beautiful embroideries with the minimum of trouble.

Wool and thread

No. 20 needle with a double strand of Broder Medicis Tapestry wool

There are many different yarns available in a wonderful range of colours. Tapestry wool and crewel wool (which is finer than tapestry wool) are both suitable, but the type used will depend on the count of the canvas. You may have to experiment to see which gives you the best coverage, and you can substitute different yarns for the ones given in the book.

I have used DMC wool and threads which are available from all good needlecraft shops. For working on 10 count canvas, you will need to use one strand of DMC Tapestry Wool. For 14 count canvas I use two strands of DMC Broder Medicis Tapestry Wool, which is the same weight as crewel wool. For working cross stitch on a 14 count canvas, I use one strand of DMC Coton Perlé No. 5.

Needles

Bead needle with strong cotton thread

You will need a tapestry needle to work on canvas. These are available in various sizes, from 14 to 26. Size 14 is the thickest, and has the largest eye. Choose a size that will pass comfortably through the holes of your canvas, with an eye large enough to allow the yarn to pass through easily. If you include beads in your design, you will need a special bead needle, which is thin enough to pass through the centre of the bead.

Beads

Seed beads or *rocailles* can be used to embellish Berlin woolwork, and wonderful effects can be achieved. They are available in a wide range of colours and finishes, and can be used to work an entire flower, or to highlight certain areas of the embroidery. If a purse or bag was being stitched, sometimes the whole of the design including the background was worked in beads.

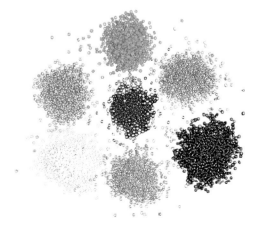

Canvas

Although the Victorians sometimes worked embroidery on even weave fabric, canvas was a much more common material. There are three main types of canvas:

Single canvas This is woven with single vertical and horizontal threads. It is sometimes difficult to use, as the stitches can become distorted because the canvas threads are not locked at their intersection.

Interlock canvas This is similar in construction to single canvas. It consists of two thin twisted vertical threads that wrap around a slightly thicker horizontal thread at the intersection, to give it extra rigidity.

Double thread, or Penelope canvas This was the first type of machine-woven canvas to be produced and is still available today. It is woven from pairs of vertical and horizontal threads, which makes it very firm to work on.

With the exception of interlock canvas, the types shown are available in a choice of colours, and this should be considered when you are working a piece of embroidery. If you are using pale shades of thread, you should use white canvas as this can be covered more easily, but a darker canvas would be a better choice if you want to use dark shades.

Canvas is measured in mesh size, the mesh being the point at which the threads intersect. A ten mesh canvas, for example, has ten threads per inch, which is the same as the number of holes. The greater the number of holes, the smaller the stitch. For ease of working, especially when you are using tapestry wool, a ten mesh interlock canvas is best. If you want to use beads, a fourteen mesh canvas may be better.

Prevent the edges of the canvas from fraying, or the wool catching on the rough threads, by binding the canvas edges with tape.

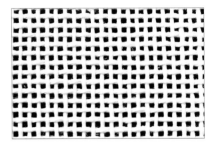

Single canvas

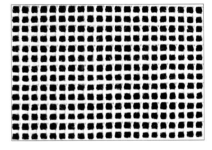

Interlock canvas

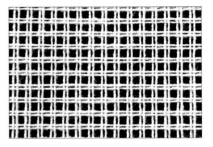

Double thread canvas

Scissors

Most embroiderers have various types of scissors as part of their personal collection of sewing items. A pair of small scissors with sharp points should be used for cutting embroidery threads, and you will need a pair of dressmaking scissors for canvas.

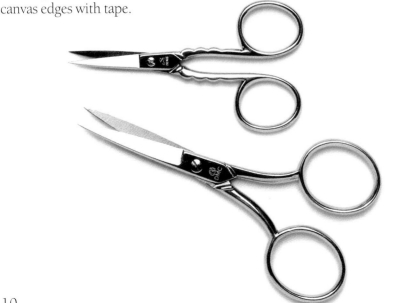

Frames

Frames are available in all shapes and sizes, the simplest being a stretcher frame which is made from four pieces of wood which are joined at the corners. The size of your frame will depend on your piece of work. Make sure you allow enough canvas to keep your working area well clear of the inner edge of the frame; the canvas can then be tacked or stapled on to it.

Rotating (slate) frames offer more versatility, as they can be adjusted to fit the size of the design. These frames have lengths of wood at the top and bottom, which have a circular profile and webbing attached. Two side bars have slots, into which the lengths of wood are secured with a nut or screw. To use, tack the canvas to the webbing on the top and bottom sections, and assemble the frame. Lace your canvas to the webbing and stretch it over the frame.

My personal favourite, which I work on throughout this book, is the Able Stretcher frame. It is lightweight, strong and fully adjustable.

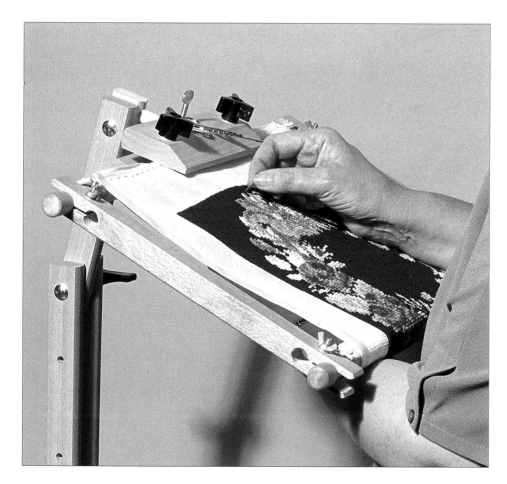

A floor-standing frame will leave your hands free to work your embroidery

11

Finishing equipment

Almost all the equipment needed for finishing your embroidery can be found around the house, or in the garage or workshop. It is important to use rustproof nails, as they will not mark your canvas when it is wet.

Blocking

This is the process of stretching and flattening a finished embroidery. You will need: a piece of **blockboard**, at least 2cm (¾in) thick, and 5–7.5cm (2–3in) larger all round than your piece of canvas; a sheet of **polythene** to cover the blockboard and prevent the wood from getting wet; a **mist spray** to dampen the canvas; some **rustproof nails** and a small **claw hammer** to secure the dampened canvas to the blockboard.

Mounting and framing

Embroideries that are to be hung on the wall should be mounted on a sheet of **hardboard**. I use **pins** to fix the canvas temporarily to the hardboard, then **thin string** to lace the sides of the canvas together on the back. Alternatively, you could use **tacks** to stretch the canvas over a **wooden stretcher**.

When the mounted canvas is framed, use **thin card** as a backing, and hold everything together with **masking tape**.

Key for photograph

1. *Masking tape*
2. *Stretcher frame*
3. *Thin card*
4. *Hardboard*
5. *Polythene sheet*
6. *Blockboard*
7. *Mist sprayer*
8. *Rustproof nails*
9. *Claw hammer*
10. *Pins/nails*
11. *Thin string*
12. *Thread*

Getting started

The projects in this book are all based on original Berlin Woolwork designs. I have chosen simple projects as well as more complicated designs that use beading and a variety of stitches, so that your work can progress gradually.

The following pages explain in detail how to start your embroidery. Even if you are new to Berlin Woolwork, you should be able to achieve a perfect result by following the step-by-step instructions.

Working with charts

All the designs in this book are *charted* i.e. they are worked from a chart as opposed to being printed on the canvas. Each square on the chart carries a symbol which represents a different colour and type of thread, stitch or bead. You should always refer to the key before starting to embroider.

Always start your embroidery in the centre of the chart (marked by the arrows). This corresponds with the point at which the horizontal and vertical lines of basting stitches cross on your canvas.

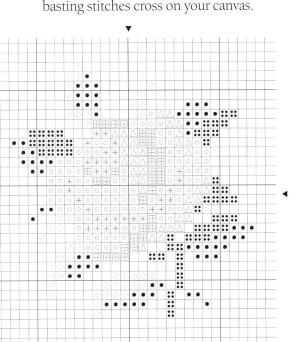

27 x 27 stitches

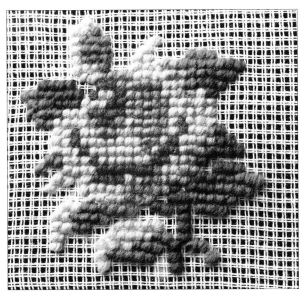

Above: motif worked in DMC Tapestry Wool on 10 count canvas.

Below: motif worked in DMC Broder Medicis on 14 count canvas

Key

colour	symbol
Light pink	△
Medium pink	▨
Dark pink	⊡
Dark green	✦
Light green	✳
Medium green	♡
Dark green	∷

Note the shade code will depend on which yarn you choose.

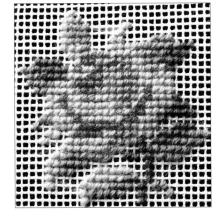

14

Preparing the canvas

Canvaswork is best worked in some kind of frame, as tension on the horizontal and vertical lines of canvas will stop the finished piece of work becoming distorted. It also means that your stitches can be worked more easily, and the end result will be much neater than a hand-held piece of embroidery. The easiest frame to use is probably the slate frame, as when you use this with a floor stand, it leaves both hands free to embroider.

1. Cut the canvas to size, then fold two opposite sides together to find the centre. Repeat with the remaining two sides.

2. Mark the horizontal and vertical centre lines with basting stitches. Bind all sides of the canvas with masking tape.

3. Fasten the canvas to the webbing using tacking stitches top and bottom.

Mounting the canvas on a slate frame

Match the centre of the edge of your canvas to the centre of the webbing and stitch the canvas to the frame at the top and bottom edges. Roll sufficient canvas over the rods at the top and bottom of the frame to ensure that you have the correct size to work on. Adjust the wing nuts at the corners to hold it in place.

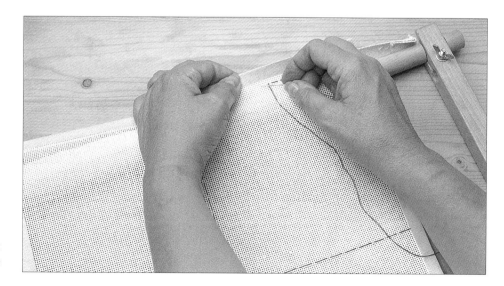

Stitching the canvas to the frame

Fixing canvas to a stretcher

A stretcher frame is the ideal way to keep your canvas stretched as you work your embroidery. It need not be expensive: if you have a budget to keep to, you can use an old picture frame, or even make your own from off-cuts of wood that you have lying around.

1. Fold the canvas round the frame, then pin the middle of one side to the frame.

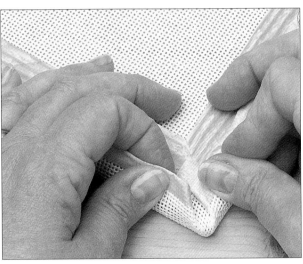

2. Fold and pin the middle of the opposite side, then pin the other two sides in the same way. Fold the corners.

3. Pin the corners.

Preparing the yarn

Do not use a length of wool that is more than 38cm (15in); it will soon begin to fray because of the roughness of the canvas. If you have a large area to stitch, it is easier to cut several lengths and hang them over your frame before you start.

DMC Tapestry wool
Pull the wool from the skein and cut it into 40cm (15in) lengths.

Broder Medicis tapestry wool
1. Remove the wrappers, untwist the skein and cut the knot.

2. Pull the strand from the skein and cut two equal lengths.

Threading needles

DMC Tapestry Wool
Threading the wool on to the needle using a slip of paper.

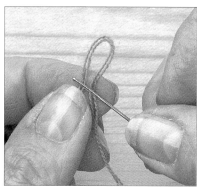

Broder Medicis tapestry wool
Threading the needle with a loop of wool.

Stitches

I am including only four embroidery stitches in this section: cross stitch, tent stitch, velvet stitch and Gobelin straight stitch, which has been used for backgrounds. The Victorian needlewoman sometimes used other canvas work stitches, but the main stitches used were cross stitch, tent stitch and velvet stitch.

Working the embroidery

The most important point to remember when starting your embroidery is to make sure that the design is positioned in the centre of the canvas, so you have enough canvas around the edge to finish the project.

To place the design correctly, mark the canvas horizontally and vertically (see the examples on pages 22-23) with a row of basting stitches. Use this as a guide for matching the centre of the canvas to the centre of the chart.

It is a matter of preference where you begin to embroider. Some like to start in the centre, while others start at the bottom and work upwards. Either is acceptable, as long as you have counted the threads and the squares on the chart carefully. Tent stitch and cross stitch should be worked from right to left and velvet stitch from left to right, leaving the background until last.

Tent stitch

This is one of the oldest embroidery stitches, and has several names. Worked on very fine canvas it is called *petit point* and on coarser canvas *gros point*. It is also known as half cross stitch or needlepoint.

Work across the canvas from left to right. Make a diagonal stitch over one thread of single thread canvas (single canvas) or one block of double thread canvas (double or tapestry canvas) in each direction. A piece which is to be worked in tent stitch should always be held in a frame to reduce the risk of distortion, as the stitch pulls only in one direction.

If the finished work is to be used for a chair seat or cushion, it may be strengthened by tramming. This is done on a double thread canvas, by laying a length of wool horizontally on the canvas and working the stitch over it.

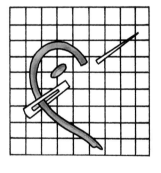

Four strands of Broder Medicis over one thread of 14 count interlock canvas in each direction.

DMC Tapestry Wool on 10 count double thread canvas over one pair of threads in each direction.

Coton Perlé No. 5 over one thread of 14 count interlock canvas in each direction.

Cross stitch

This is probably the most popular embroidery stitch today. For the best results, work on double thread canvas and complete each stitch before moving on to the next. The result is a neat, raised cross stitch which cannot be achieved by working in rows. The canvas will not distort because the stitch is pulled in both directions, so you do not have to use a frame and can just hold your work in your hand if you prefer.

The stitch consists of two diagonal stitches over two threads of single canvas in each direction, or one hole of double or tapestry canvas. Make sure that all the diagonal stitches on top go in the same direction.

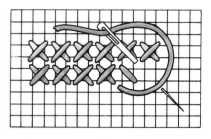

working cross stitch

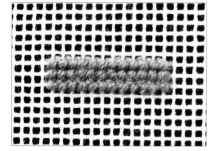

Two strands of Broder Medicis over one thread of 14 count interlock canvas in each direction.

DMC Tapestry Wool over one pair of threads of 10 count double thread canvas in each direction.

Coton Perlé No.5 over two threads of 14 count interlock canvas in each direction.

Gobelin straight stitch

This is very simple, and consists of straight stitches worked in vertical rows over the desired number of threads. On second and subsequent rows, the top of each stitch is worked into the same hole as the bottom of the stitch on the row above. It is ideal for backgrounds because it is easy to work and large areas can be covered very quickly.

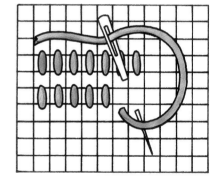

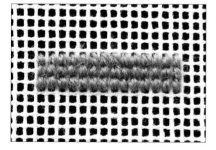

Two strands of Broder Medicis over one thread of 14 count interlock canvas.

DMC Tapestry Wool over two pairs of threads of 10 count double thread canvas.

Note

There is no third example of this stitch because the backgrounds throughout this book are worked only in DMC Tapestry Wool or Broder Medicis tapestry wool.

19

Velvet stitch

This was originally called pile or plush stitch, and was used to create areas of interest in the embroidery. Sometimes the loops of wool were left extra-long and then professionally clipped to create a sculpted effect. It is sufficient, however, to leave a small loop which can be clipped to give a slightly raised effect.

Start at the bottom edge of the canvas and work upwards, following the diagram and working the stitch from left to right.

Bring your needle out through the canvas and insert it again two threads to the right and two threads up, making a diagonal stitch.

Bring the needle out again at the starting hole. Form a loop of yarn either by holding it in place with your thumb, or working it over a gauge such as a knitting needle, and insert the needle again in the hole at the top of the first stitch.

Bring the needle out again two horizontal threads below this hole, underneath your first loop. Finally, make a diagonal stitch over the top of your loop, entering the canvas two threads to the left and two threads up, and finish by bringing the needle out through the hole where your last stitch started, ready to make the next stitch.

Cut through the loops of wool or cotton and trim the pile to the required length.

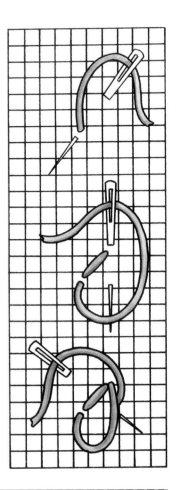

Two strands of Broder Medicis over one thread of 14 count interlock canvas in each direction.

One strand of DMC Tapestry Wool over one pair of threads of 10 count double canvas in each direction.

One strand of Coton Perlé No.5 over one thread of 14 count interlock canvas in each direction.

Beading

Beads were usually used in Berlin Woolwork to embroider flowers or a particular area of the design, instead of working it in cross stitch.

Embroiderers today can choose from a wide range of beads, but the most suitable type for Berlin Woolwork is a *rocaille*, or seed bead. These are round glass beads which are available in a variety of finishes, including antique, frosted, opaque and irridescent. A 14 count canvas should be used when you are stitching your design in beads.

Working with beads

You will need a bead needle, sewing cotton in a slightly lighter shade than the bead you want to use, and a small container for the beads so they can be picked up easily by the needle. If you are using more than one type of bead you will need several containers.

Method

Begin by fastening the first bead to your work using one or two back stitches. Bring the needle out at the bottom left-hand corner of the square you plan to sew the bead over (point A on the diagram below).

With the needle, pick a bead from the container. Insert the needle again at the top right-hand corner so that the bead is held in place with a half cross stitch (see point B on the diagram below).

When you have finished the beading, finish off by working two or three back stitches to secure your thread.

14 count interlock canvas, enlarged for clarity.

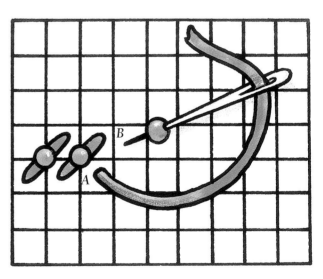

Starting to stitch

Do not knot the wool when you start to stitch, as this will make a bump on the back of your work. Instead, leave a length of wool to the right side of your work, just in front of where your stitches will lie, and hold it in place by stitching over it.

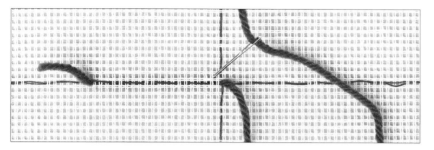

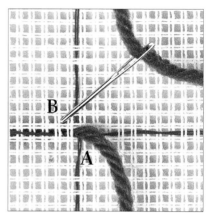

1. Take the needle through the front of the canvas on one of the centre lines, about 5cm (2in) from the centre point. Bring the needle and wool back up to the front at the centre point A. Start the first stitch by taking the needle down through the canvas at point B.

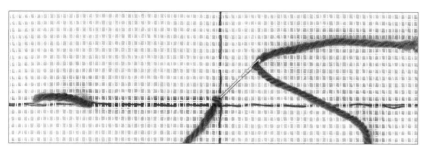

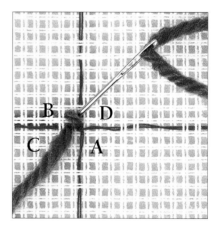

2. Complete the first stitch by bringing the needle up through the hole at point C, then down again at point D, enclosing the length of wool on the underside of the canvas.

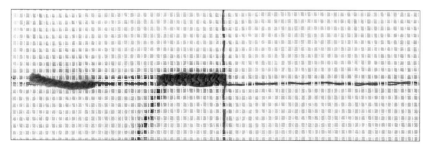

3. Continue making stitches along the centre line.

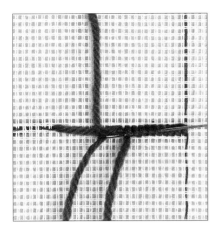

4. When you reach the end of the row, turn the work over, take the needle and wool through four or five stitches to anchor the tail, then trim off the excess.

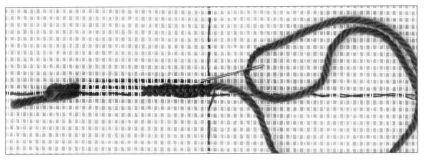

5. Repeat step 1 to start the second row of stitches, then repeat steps 2–4 for the required length.

Stitching a block of solid colour

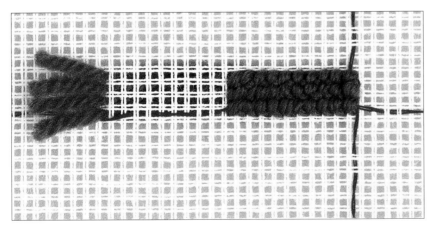

Blocks of the same colour should be worked in rows, all of which should be sewn in the same direction, and the thread tied off at the end.

Stitching random areas

Sets of contoured stitches in the same colour should be worked consecutively until the thread runs out.

Finishing techniques

As the reverse of your work should be neat and tidy, finish off by threading the wool through a few stitches. If you are carrying a thread from one area to another, you should not leave a long loop. Instead, the wool should be fastened off and started again in the new area.

Blocking

Canvaswork should always be blocked, even when the embroidery has been worked in a frame. You will need the items shown on page 12.

1. Make small cuts along the selvedge so that your work will stretch evenly.

2. Cover the blockboard with a clear plastic sheet and place the canvas face up on top.

3. Dampen the canvas all over with a mist spray.

4. Hammer a nail into the top centre of the canvas. Pulling the work gently, hammer another nail into the bottom centre, making sure the threads are straight. Repeat the process at each side, making sure that the vertical and horizontal threads cross at right angles as well as being straight.

5. Hammer more nails around the outside at 2cm (¾in) intervals, making sure that the embroidery remains damp at all times. Leave to dry and remove the nails.

25

Mounting

When you have spent many hours embroidering a piece of work, it is well worth spending time mounting it carefully, as it provides the perfect finishing touch.

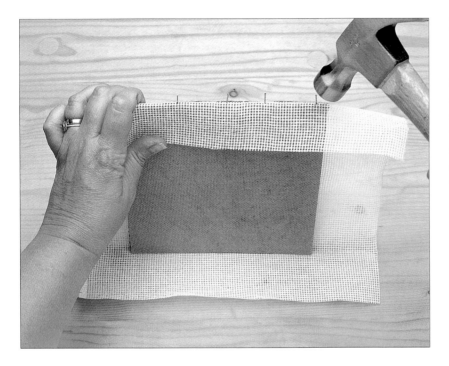

Mounting on hardboard

1. Cut a piece of hardboard the same size as the finished embroidery, and place the work over it, with the right side of the work facing you. Fold the top edge of the canvas on to the back of the hardboard, then secure it in position with pins inserted into the top edge of the hardboard.

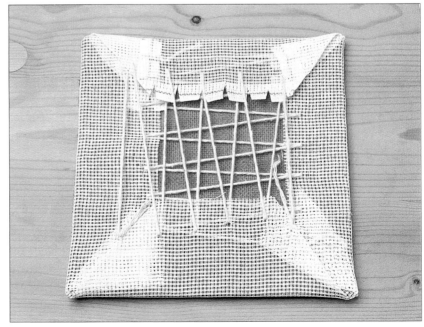

2. Fold and secure the bottom of the canvas in a similar way. Mitre the corners in the same way as when mounting canvas on a stretcher frame (see page 16), and lace the top and bottom edges together with thin string, making sure the canvas is stretched evenly. Repeat the process for the two side edges.

Framing

When choosing your frame, make sure it is in keeping with the embroidery as well as your decor. The inside opening should always be slightly smaller than the mount so that the recess of the inside of the frame will fit over the edge of the embroidery and hold it in place. Back the embroidery with a piece of thick card held in place with panel pins, and stick masking tape along the join between the frame and the card.

Close-up of the corner

The framed embroidery

Embroideries

The first three embroideries are very small so they are ideal first projects. I hope they will whet your appetite and encourage you to develop your skills further. All three are worked in the same way, in cross stitch over one hole of canvas in each direction using two strands of Broder Medicis wool. The areas round each design, which you can just see in the photographs, are worked in Gobelin stitch.

Before starting each embroidery, prepare the canvas as shown on page 15. Following the steps on pages 16-17, mount the canvas in a frame and prepare the wool.

You will need

For each embroidery:
a small piece of 14 count single thread interlock canvas, approximate size 12.5 x 16cm (5 x 6¼in)
DMC Broder Medicis wool in the colours shown in the relevant keys
Tapestry needle No. 20

Poppy

These bright flowers make a real impact in the fields in summer, though they usually live for just a day.

Key

code	colour	symbol
8135	Pink	♡
8102	Dark red	◖
8666	Light red	•˙
8346	Dark green	⊞
8342	Medium green	◁
8341	Light green	⊙
Noir	Black	◻

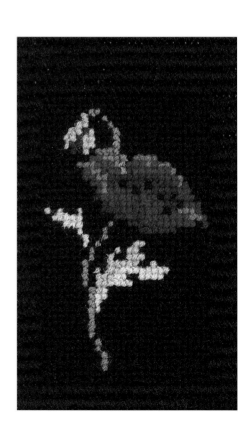

Harebell spray

Flowering from midsummer to early autumn, this delicate pale blue flower with its slender stem grows in grassy places as well as on dunes and heathland.

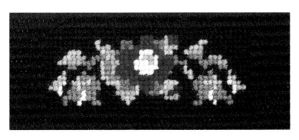

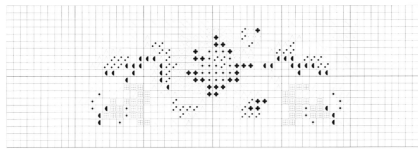

Key

code	colour	symbol
8135	Pink	◇
8102	Dark red	✚
8666	Light red	♡
8748	Yellow	•
8895	Dark mauve	⊞
8896	Light mauve	◿
8346	Dark green	◖
8342	Medium green	••
8341	Light green	△
Noir	Black	◻

Hydrangea spray

This shrub came originally from Japan. Its dense clusters of showy flowers need extra care to cope with our colder climate.

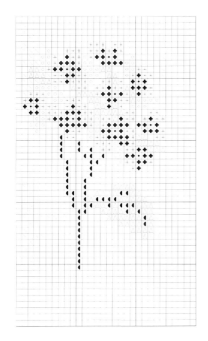

Key

code	colour	symbol
8899	Dark blue	✚
8798	Light blue	✳
8748	Yellow	•
8346	Dark green	◖
8342	Medium green	△
8341	Light green	○
Black	Noir	◻

29

Violet and rose spray

This beautiful posy includes violets and roses, two favourite flowers of the Victorians. The design is a little more advanced, but it is worked in the same stitches and wool as the small projects on the previous pages.

Before starting to embroider, prepare the canvas as shown on page 15. Then following the steps on pages 16-17, mount the canvas in a frame and prepare the wool.

You will need

14 count single thread interlock canvas 18 x 19cm (7 x 7½in)
DMC Broder Medicis wool - colours as shown in the key
Tapestry needle No. 20

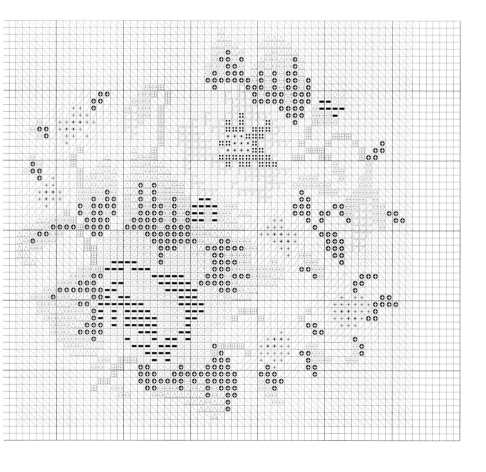

Key

code	colour	symbol
8720	Dark blue	⠿
8899	Medium blue	◺
8798	Light blue	◿
8135	Pink	♡
8102	Dark red	▬
8666	Light red	◇
8748	Yellow	⊙
8895	Dark mauve	✳
8896	Light mauve	◿
8346	Dark green	✦
8342	Medium green	⊖
8341	Light green	△
8109	Brown	⊞
Noir	Black	◺

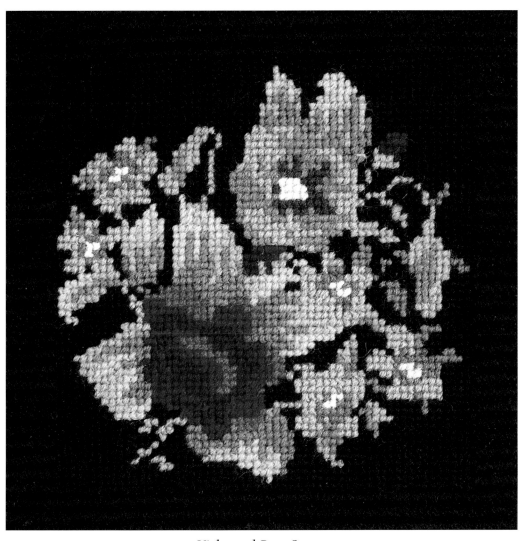

Violet and Rose Spray
Motif shown larger than full size
of 10 x 10.5cm (4in x 4¼in)

Floral wreath

This delightful combination of roses, lilies and auricula is worked in cross stitch with a dark blue background. The example measures about 30cm (11¾in) square, and was worked in tapestry wool on 10 count double thread tapestry canvas over one double thread in each direction.

Before starting to embroider, prepare the canvas as shown on page 15. Then following the steps on pages 16-17, mount the canvas in a frame and prepare the wool.

You will need

10 count double thread canvas 40cm (15½in) square

DMC Tapestry Wool in the colours shown in the key

Tapestry needle No.20

Floral wreath
Shown less than full size of
30cm (11¾in) square

Key to chart opposite

code	colour	symbol	code	colour	symbol	code	colour	symbol
7049	Light yellow	⊡	7361	Medium green	★	7210	Dark pink	▽
7431	Medium yellow	●	7362	Dark green	⊞	7853	Light peach	⊕
7726	Dark yellow	⊖	7800	Light blue	♡	7011	Medium peach	⊠
7024	Light mauve	↔	7035	Medium blue	▲	7007	Dark peach	✚
7025	Medium mauve	═	7314	Dark blue	▬	Ecru	Cream	◦
7026	Dark mauve	◖	7133	Light pink	◻	7023	Navy	◹
7422	Light green	◇	7204	Medium pink	⁘			

33

Lily of the Valley

A favourite of great grandmothers, lily of the valley can be found growing in a shady corner of the garden in early spring. Its delicate perfume and simple bell-shaped flowers are always welcomed with delight after the long, cold winter.

This design is worked in cross stitch over one double thread of canvas in each direction, using one strand of tapestry wool.

Before starting to embroider, prepare the canvas as shown on page 15. Following the steps on pages 16-17, mount the canvas in a frame and prepare the wool.

You will need

10 count double canvas, size 30 x 30cm (11¾ x 11¾in)
DMC Tapestry Wool in the colours shown in the key
Tapestry needle No.20

Key

code	colour	symbol
Blanc	White	◺
7746	Cream	✳
7141	Light beige	○
7463	Medium beige	⊟
7465	Dark beige	⊞
7060	Darkest beige	⦂
7549	Light green	♡
7548	Medium green	●
7547	Dark green	◇
7044	Darkest green	◖
Noir	Black	◿

Lily of the Valley
Convallaria majalis
Shown less than full size of
19cm (7½in) square

Pansy

A favourite flower of the Victorians, the hardy pansy with its striking face-like markings, bright colours and subtle scent, was used in table-top arrangements which adorned the banqueting tables of great houses.

This design is worked in cross stitch over one hole of canvas in each direction, using one strand of Coton Perlé for the leaves and two strands of Broder Medicis tapestry wool for the flowers, with beaded accents.

Before starting to embroider, prepare the canvas as shown on page 15. Then following the steps on pages 16-17, frame the canvas and prepare the wool.

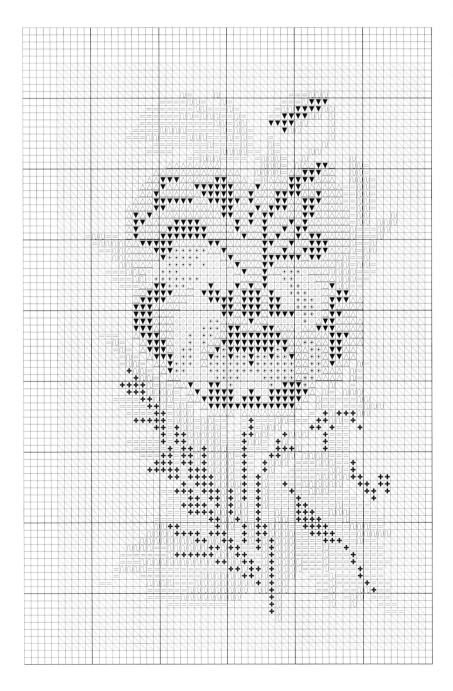

You will need

14 count single thread interlock canvas 18 x 23cm (7 x 9in)
DMC Broder Medicis tapestry wool (see key)
DMC Coton Perlé No.5
DMC v1 general seed beads (see key)
Tapestry needle No.20
Bead needle

Key

code	colour	symbol
Broder Medicis		
8895	Dark mauve	▼
8896	Medium mauve	△
8397	Light mauve	○
Noir	Black	◻
Coton Perlé		
469	Dark green	✚
471	Medium green	◡
472	Light green	=
General seed beads		
06307	Yellow	⊙

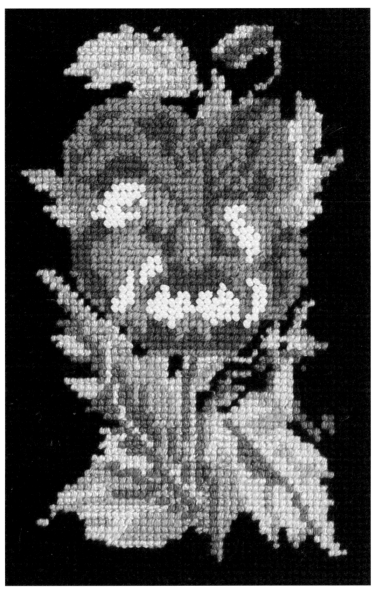

Pansy

Viola wittrockiana

Full size

Fuchsia

These beautiful shrubs, which are available in many varieties, are named after the 16th-century German botanist Leonhard Fuchs. The exotic blooms were probably grown on a grand scale as Victorian greenhouse plants, and displayed outside only in the summer months to protect them from frost.

This design is worked in cross stitch over one thread of canvas in each direction, using one strand of Coton Perlé, and two strands of Broder Medicis tapestry wool.

Before starting to embroider, prepare the canvas as shown on page 15. Then following the steps on pages 16-17, mount the canvas in a frame and prepare the yarn.

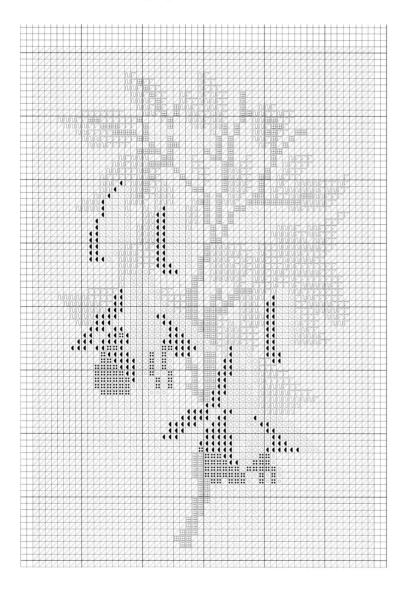

You will need

14 count single thread interlock canvas 18 x 23cm (7 x 9in)
DMC Broder Medicis wool in the colours shown in the key
DMC Coton Perlé No.5 (see key)
DMC beads (see key):
  v1 general seed beads
  v3 metallic beads
  v2 nostalgia beads
Tapestry needle No. 20
Bead needle

Key

code	colour	symbol
Broder Medicis		
8419	Medium green	〇
8420	Light green	⬚
Noir	Black	⬚
Coton Perlé		
915	Dark magenta	◖
718	Medium magenta	⬚
3609	Light magenta	◇
General seed beads		
053746 lilac	Light mauve	○
Metallic beads		
05333 purple	Dark mauve	⠿
Nostalgia beads		
033345 olive green	Dark green	⊞

Fuchsia
F. Magellanica
Full size

Poppies

The red, pink, orange, yellow and cream shades of the poppy, with its willowy stems and delicate flowers, was a joy to behold in the Victorian garden. Wide flower borders, planted with different varieties of poppy, made a dazzling display on a hot summer day.

The design is worked over one thread of canvas in each direction using one strand of Coton Perlé and two strands of Broder Medicis wool. Before starting to embroider, prepare the canvas as shown on page 15. Following the steps on pages 16-17, frame the canvas and prepare the wool.

You will need

14 count single thread interlock canvas, 18 x 23cm (7 x 9in)

DMC Broder Medicis tapestry wool (see key)

DMC Coton Perlé No.5 (see key)

DMC beads (see key):
v1 general seed beads
v3 metallic beads
v4 frosted beads

Tapestry needle No.20

Bead needle

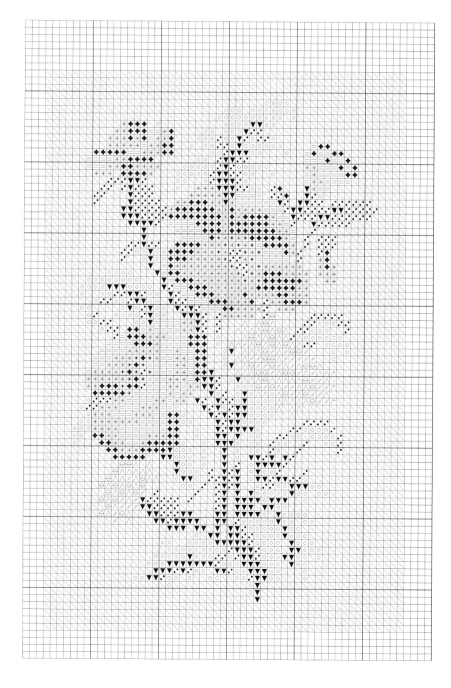

Key

code	colour	symbol
Broder Medicis		
8420	Light green	⊙
8419	Medium green	⦂
Noir	Black	◱
Coton Perlé		
3325	Light blue	△
334	Medium blue	⊖
312	Dark blue	⊠
General seed beads		
02816 Wine Red	Light red	▤
02326 Light Clover	Medium red	✳
03469 Moss Green	Dark green	▼
Metallic beads		
02814 Wine Red	Dark red	✚
Frosted beads		
12310	Black	◉

Poppy
Papaver sp.
Full size

Bluebells

With its bell-shaped flowers, heady perfume and graceful appearance, this flower is a familiar sight, carpeting the woodland with blue in late spring. In the Victorian garden border, it would have grown alongside lily of the valley and other spring flowers.

This design is worked in cross stitch over one thread of canvas in each direction, using one strand of Coton Perlé, and two strands of crewel weight wool.

Before starting to embroider, prepare the canvas as shown on page 15. Then following the steps on pages 16-17, frame the canvas and prepare the wool.

You will need

14 count single thread interlock canvas 18 x 23cm (7 x 9in)

DMC Broder Medicis tapestry wool (see key)

DMC Coton Perlé No.5 (see key)

DMC beads (see key):
v1 general seed beads
v3 metallic beads
v4 frosted beads

Tapestry needle No.20

Bead needle

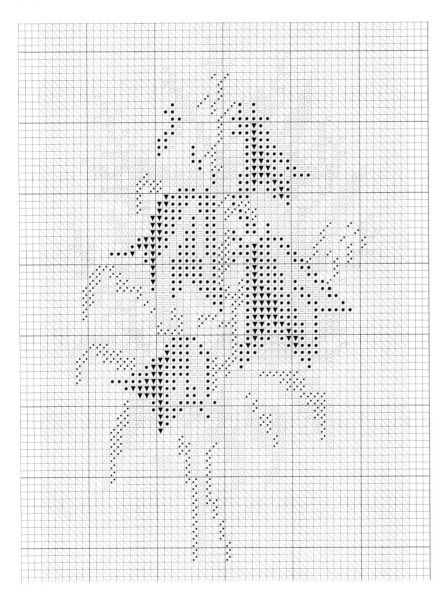

Key

Code	colour	symbol
Broder Medicis		
8411	Light green	◇
8422	Dark green	•
Noir	Black	◻
Coton Perlé		
718	Medium magenta	♡
General seed beads		
04794	Mid blue	●
Metallic beads		
04930	Dark blue	▼
Deep blue		
Frosted beads		
04800	Light blue	⊟
Baby blue		

Bluebell
Endymion non-scriptus
Full size

Beaded pink rose

Perhaps the doyenne of all British flowers, the rose has many varieties. Old garden roses were very popular in Victorian times. Double-headed, in subtle shades of pink, crimson and white, they had a heady perfume which made them popular for making pot pourri.

This design is worked in cross stitch over one thread of canvas in each direction, using two strands of crewel weight wool. The background is cream, and the flowers are worked completely in beads.

Before starting to embroider, prepare the canvas as shown on page 15. Following the steps on pages 16-17, frame the canvas and prepare the wool.

You will need

14 count single thread interlock canvas 24 x 23cm (9½ x 9in)
DMC Broder Medicis tapestry wool (see key)
DMC v1 general seed beads in the colours shown in key
Tapestry needle No.20
Bead needle

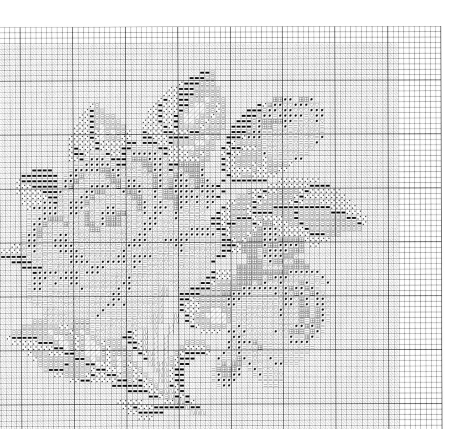

Key

code	colour	symbol
Broder Medicis		
8419	Light green	
8412	Medium green	
8413	Dark green	
8414	Darkest green	
ecru	Cream	
8501	Light brown	
8120	Dark brown	
General seed beads		
01819 (very pale pink)	Lightest pink	
01818 (ice pink)	Light pink	
13713 (pale rose)	Medium pink	
01776 (salmon pink)	Dark pink	
02326 (light clover)	Darkest pink	

Pink rose
Full size

Floral spray

This exuberant design of roses, violets and phlox incorporates beading and velvet stitch to provide interesting texture. It is worked in cross stitch over one thread of canvas in each direction, using one strand of Coton Perlé and two strands of Broder Medicis. The areas round the design, which you can see in the photograph, are in Gobelin stitch.

Before starting to embroider, prepare the canvas as shown on page 15. Following the steps on pages 16-17, frame the canvas and prepare the wool.

Note: the key to this design can be found on page 48

You will need

14 count single thread interlock canvas 26 x 23cm (10 x 9in)

DMC Broder Medicis tapestry wool (see key)

DMC Coton Perlé No.5

DMC beads: v1 general seed beads; v2 nostalgia beads; v3 metallic beads

Tapestry needle No. 20

Bead needle

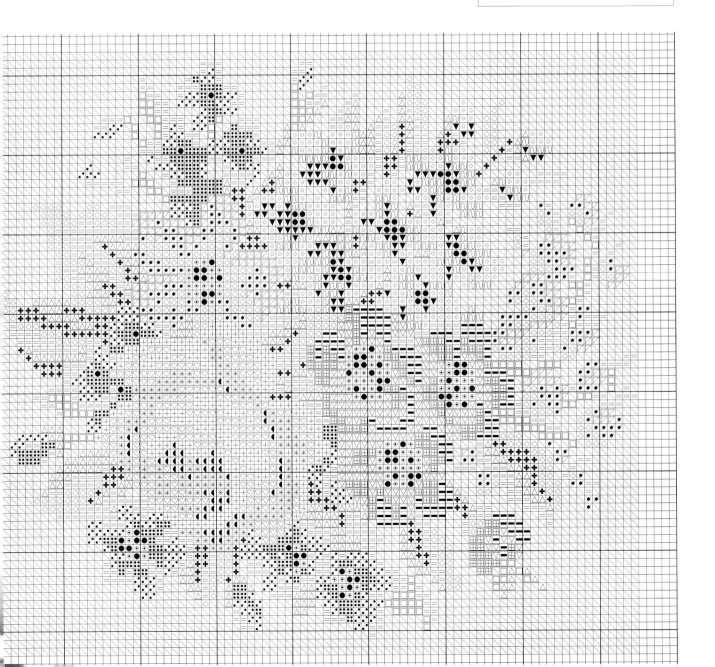